# Don't Write off our Rhinos!

**Dedicated to all the Rhino Warriors who are contributing and working hard to keep our rhinos safe.**

Compiled by Donna Grimsley

Cover Design by Sradha Vadher

Published by Dolman Scott in 2018

Book:      978-1-911412-76-2
iBooks:    978-1-911412-77-9
Kindle:    978-1-911412-78-6


Dolman Scott Ltd
www.dolmanscott.co.uk

# CONTENTS

# INTRODUCTION

This book was inspired by my passion to save the rhinos in South Africa. The idea was to create awareness about rhino poaching around the world while encouraging children (and adults!) to get creative by writing about rhinos. I believe it is so important for us to make the young people of today aware of how essential it is to protect our wildlife. Without our protection the magic we experience in the bush today may disappear forever. Raising awareness and funds for anti-poaching efforts in The Pilanesberg National Park is the ultimate goal of the *Writing For Rhinos* project.

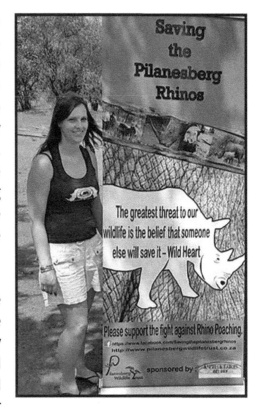

I have chosen to support The Pilanesberg Wildlife Trust because I value the work that they do. I have been visiting The Pilanesberg National Park for many years, each time experiencing something new and unique. In 2012 my father, Vaughan Brown, was invited to attend a rhino notching. Unfortunately my father was unable to attend. Darryn, my husband, and I went in his place. It was on this weekend that I met Lee Dormer, Perry and Steve Dell for the first time. Lee spoke to me about what was happening to the rhinos in The Pilanesberg National Park. He explained to me how they were being poached and what the team in Pilanesberg were doing to help prevent this. I immediately wanted to be part of the enormous effort to save the rhinos in Pilanesberg National Park. It was then that I started to make items such as bracelets, necklaces and key rings to sell in order to raise funds for rhino protection. Luckily my mother, Bev Brown, has always been very creative and crafty and we worked together to make magnets and other items to sell at market days and at Pilanesberg Centre on some weekends. My mom soon came up with the initiative 'Take a Shot for the Rhino' which has been extremely successful at all fundraisers!

In July 2016 my husband and I moved to the U.K. I could no longer visit the park on the weekends to raise funds. Thankfully my parents, Perry and The Makanyane Volunteers have continued to 'set up shop' outside The Pilanesberg Centre and fundraising continues and is more frequent than ever! I found it really hard being so far from Pilanesberg and I felt quite helpless not being able to be as involved as I used to be. I was interested to hear that not many people in the U.K were aware of the rhino poaching crisis. I then started to think about how I could create more awareness and the *Writing For Rhinos* project was born.

The generosity and enthusiasm of everyone involved has been extraordinary. A huge THANK YOU to Laurel Allen from Southern California who made an extremely generous donation which meant we did not have to worry about publishing or distribution costs. 100% of all funds raised through entry fees and book sales go to The Pilanesberg Wildlife Trust for their anti-poaching efforts.

I hope you enjoy the book!

Donna

# WHAT IS RHINO POACHING AND WHY DOES IT HAPPEN?

Rhino poaching is the illegal practice of trespassing on another's property to hunt a rhino and remove it's horn, often killing the rhino in the process. Sometimes the rhino is shot first, sometimes the rhino's horn is hacked off while the rhino is still alive and sometimes the rhino stays alive long after it's face as been left with big gaping holes resulting in immense pain and suffering. This is the reality of rhino poaching.

The demand for Rhino horn has escalated in recent years due to its popularity in Asian countries, especially Vietnam. It is used in Traditional Chinese Medicine, but increasingly common is its use as a status symbol to display success and wealth.

While it is believed that rhino horn holds medicinal properties the fact of the matter is that rhino horn is made up of the same materials as human fingernails and hair. There is no scientific evidence to support the claim that rhino horn has medicinal properties.

# WHY I HAVE CHOSEN TO SUPPORT THE PILANESBERG WILDLIFE TRUST?

The Pilanesberg Wildlife Trust funds a designated anti-poaching unit in The Pilanesberg National Park. Due to restricted resources they rely heavily on donations to ensure the rhinos in the park are kept as safe as possible. The park is very lucky to have two tracking dogs who are specially trained to track poached rhinos and poachers. The fight against rhino poaching has proven to be a hard and frustrating one. While the team is continuously updating their resources and knowledge, it often seems that the poachers are one step ahead. Despite this fact, the team remains motivated and determined to get up early and stay out late and put their lives on the line to do their best to protect the rhinos in Pilanesberg National Park. In addition to all the hands on work involved with keeping the rhinos safe, the Pilaneserg Wildlife Trust is also very much involved with the community surrounding Pilanesberg. The Pilanesberg Wildlife Trust promotes the upliftment of the communities in the related fields of Nature Conservation and Tourism. The PWT helps to create feelings of ownership and pride of the Park within the local community, including the young children. Wildlife Clubs and taking people into the park to experience the wonders of wildlife is part of what the PWT facilitates. PWT also visits schools to talk to the pupils about the interdependence of humans and nature.

My values and beliefs align with what the Pilanesberg Wildlife Trust sets out to achieve. Through education and creating love and respect for wildlife we can ensure its protection. Perry Dell is the passionate manager of The Pilanesberg Wildlife Trust. She has always been forthcoming in sharing what the funds we raise are used for. I know and trust that the funds we raise are spent in the best way possible. This is why I have chosen to support The Pilanesberg Wildlife Trust.

Please visit **pilanesbergwildlifetrust.co.za** for more information.

# ACKNOWLEDGEMENTS

There may be a certain nobility in being an unsung hero, but I would prefer to give a massive shout out to all the people who have been involved in keeping our rhinos safe. First of all I would like to thank each and every person who took the time to write their rhino story and make their rhino picture. Without your enthusiasm and involvement there would be no book to publish! Thank you to Laurel Allen for your extremely generous donation to cover all publishing and distribution costs. You definitely saved me from many sleepless nights! Thank you Bakubung Bush Lodge for your contribution to the publishing costs of the book and for your continuous support with helping the rhinos in The Pilanesberg.

Much gratitude to Perry and Steve Dell who have always given their best efforts to keep our rhinos safe. Without your determination and energy the rhinos in Pilanesberg would have no hope. You inspire your teams and those around you to stand up for The Pilanesberg Rhinos. You have made it possible for us to be involved in helping to save the rhinos and have always kept us up to date with what the money we raised has been spent on. Our world needs more people like you!

In the hero stakes, they don't come better qualified than Vaughan and Beverley Brown. They have been my inspiration and biggest supporters in my journey to help save the rhinos. There are no words that can explain how much I appreciate all the hard work, sponsorships and donations, bracelet, keyring and magnet making, early mornings and advice!

Thanks too, to Darryn Grimsley, my husband, for the love, patience and support, pamphlet making and endless designing, early mornings and long drives! Thank you to Mark Brown for all the editing and advice. Thanks to Michael Catterson who advertised this project on his radio station and has given much airtime to the important issue of rhino poaching. A massive THANK YOU to the talented artist, Sradha Vadher , who has contributed some amazing illustrations for our book. You gave our book exactly what it needed!

In closing, a MASSIVE 'thank you' to **YOU** for purchasing this book. 100% of all money raised through the purchase of this book is donated to The Pilanesberg Wildlife Trust to assist with rhino protection efforts. You have made a difference and have helped to SAVE OUR RHINOS.

# A LITTLE BIT ABOUT PILANESBERG NATIONAL PARK

Pilanesberg National Park is a game reserve only three hours' drive away from South Africa's largest city (Johannesburg). The park exists in a transition zone between the dryness of the Kalahari and the wet Lowveld vegetation. This rich transitional zone attracts an incredible variety of game animals, flora and fauna that are not often found living side by side. Virtually all of the animal species native to Southern Africa can be found here, including the Big 5, Wild Dog, Roan, Tsessebe, Sable Antelope and more than 360 species of bird.

One of the best aspects of The Pilanesberg National Park is that you have the opportunity to immerse yourself in the natural world, in one of Pilanesberg's concealed photographic hides. Hidden within the park, these well-built hides provide a comfortable place to wait for that perfect photo. The hides offer rare opportunity to view the wildlife and birds in their natural habitat, safely out of sight. Two of my personal favourites are the hides at Mankwe and Ratlogo Dams.

Within the Pilanesberg National Park there are many options for accommodation. You could choose to camp, stay in a chalet, hotel or a luxury lodge.

Interestingly, Pilanesberg National Park is set within the crater of an ancient volcano, formed 1.2 billion years ago by overflowing magma. The landscape and rock formations we see today are the enduring reminders of this magnificent occurrence.

To sum it up, Pilanesberg National Park is a piece of heaven on Earth, guaranteed to leave a lasting impression on your heart and memories to last a lifetime.

# Rhino Poem

The Rhino is sad because he hasn't got any bagpipes.

The Rhino is wearing a kilt.

The rhino is playing drums.

The Rhino is Scottish because he has Scottish traditions.

The Rhino has a tartan horn.

The Rhino eats haggis.

The rhino is called Craig.

By **Max** (United Kingdom)

Illustration by **Sradha Vadher**

**Seth Breedt**, South Africa

**The Rhino is big.**

**The Rhino is huge.**

**The Rhino is Grey.**

**The Rhino has a horn.**

**The Rhino is sad.**

**The Rhino is endangered.**

By **Harvey M** (United Kingdom)

# Did You Know...

Rhinos usually give birth to one calf at a time but sometimes they have twins!

Calves stay with their moms for the first 2 to 4 years of their lives.

The gestation period of a rhino is between 15 and 16 months.

White rhino calves usually weigh more than black rhino calves at birth.

During a fight, white rhino calves will run in front of their mothers while black rhino calves will run behind their mothers.

Baby rhinos are called calves.

# HOW RHINO GOT HIS HORN

By **Rayden Breedt** (South Africa)

Once upon a time there was a big fire in the bush. When Ronnie, the baby rhino, woke up all the grass was gone so Ronnie's mommy took him for a walk to find food. Ronnie's tummy started grumbling. He was getting hungry. After a while Ronnie got so hungry that he started chewing his nails until there was nearly nothing left.

The next morning when Ronnie woke up his head was sore so he asked his mommy if he could go to the water hole to drink some water. Ronnie finally reached the water hole. He stuck his head into the water and he felt so refreshed!

Ronnie's friend, Sandy, the lion cub came up to the water hole very quietly. Ronnie got such a fright that he fell into the water and hit his nose on a rock! When Ronnie got out of the water it felt like his nose was pounding. Sandy took one look at him and burst out laughing because two big white bumps were coming out of his head at the top of his nose! Ronnie took one look at his reflection and ran straight home to his mother.

When Ronnie's mom saw the bumps on his head she immediately gave him a cold cloth made from leaves to put on the bumps to stop the swelling. Ronnie lay down under a tree to help him feel better but the bumps kept growing and growing so Ronnie's mommy took him to see Dr Ollie Ostrich.

The doctor examined the bumps on Ronnie's head and asked if he had been biting his nails recently because the two horns were made of the same thing that nails are made from. Ronnie thought back to the day that the bush was on fire and he was eating his nails. He asked the doctor if it was curable and the doctor told him that all he could do was take Panado for the pain.

AND THAT IS HOW THE RHINO GOT HIS HORN.

**Rayden Breedt** (South Africa)

# The Rhino made a Friend

**The Rhino made a friend because he does not have any family, they were poached. The Rhino had nowhere to live. The humans are his only friends because the humans protect him from being endangered by poachers for his horns.**

By **Harvey D** (United Kingdom)

Illustration By: **Kendra Robertson** (South Africa)

# The rhino is grey.
# The rhino is lonely.
# The rhino can drive.
# The rhino can run away from hunters.

By **Lakhan** (United Kingdom)

# VOLUNTEERS AT PILANESBERG

ev and Vaughan Brown are two of the many volunteers who help to raise funds in The Pilanesberg National Park. They are both passionate about saving the rhinos in Pilanesberg and are involved in making merchandise which is sold to raise funds for anti poaching efforts in the park.

Vaughan is a solid supporter of The Pilanesberg Wildlife Trust (PWT). He owns a factory which supplies water bottles to PWT. He has recently included a design which shows a rhino without a horn to symbolise the plight of our rhinos. These water bottles are sold at the gates to the park and at fundraisers. He also frequently joins the Makanyane volunteers in their efforts to maintain areas in the park.

Bev came up with the initiative *Take a Shot for the Rhino* which has proven to raise a huge amount of funds for the PWT. She uses her outstanding creativity to make a variety of bracelets, key rings, magnets and other merchandise which she donates to PWT. She joins other volunteers to sell all of these items at Pilanesberg Centre on fundraising days. Look out for the stall outside Pilanesberg Centre on your next visit!

# THE MAKANYANE VOLUNTEERS

The Makanyane Volunteers are a special group who help to make a difference in the Pilanesberg. Some of the volunteers assist with fundraising at Pilanesberg Centre while others take to the hands-on work in the park which includes maintaining various areas such as the hides.

## www.makanyane.org.za

*The Makanyane Volunteers fitting a solar powered borehole pump to feed the Kubu picnic site. This means one less place for the truck bowser to deliver water every day and to save the park diesel and on road maintenance etc*

# PROTECTORS

A tribute to those who risk it all

**Run, little friend.**

**Hurry up, quick now!**

**Into the arms of the heroes.**

**Night and day they fight your battles.**

**One day taken at a time.**

**Carefully strategizing,**

**Every next move.**

**Rescuing those in need.**

**Our rangers, their lives endangered,**

**Saving you with every last breath.**

Written By **Alexandra Price** (South Africa)

*Perry and Steve Dell*

# MILLIE, THE RHINO WHO COULD DANCE

Written By: Morgan Jacobs (South Africa)

There once was a rhino who loved to dance. Her name was Millie. She was the greatest ballet dancer ever in history. One day she was practising her dances: ballet, hip hop, tap, modern and contemporary. When... a little rat came past and she got a shock and tripped over her own leg. Then a person came past and saw her, she phoned the ambulance. They came and took her to the hospital. They took an X-ray and they said she had broken her leg. The doctor said she had to stay in hospital for two weeks. Millie said, "But my dance is in one week". So she had to tell her teacher she had to skip the dance.

Her mom gave her a **get well soon** card. It said:

Get well soon sweetheart. We will be here for you. Love you sweetheart.

Love,

MOMMY.

Millie got better. Her leg was fixed and she could go home.

Her teacher said 'Get ready because there is a dance competition for you'. Millie wore a beautiful costume and she did the best dance of her life.

Millie the dancing rhino lived a happy dancing life.

**The End of The Dancing RHINO STORY.**

# STANDING TALL SIDE BY SIDE

May the grass be long to hide you
And  the wind carry away your scent

May the dust settle to cover your tracks
And the oxpecker on your back cry loud to warn you

May your feet be ready to carry you swiftly

And the shadows hide you the next full moon
May the education of your being be far reaching

May the world be listening

And may we all protect you

Written By
**Camilla Jacobs** (South Africa)

# RHINO NOTCHING AND DNA COLLECTION IN PILANESBERG

The response is "If we were not doing what we can, would the numbers of poached Rhinos be greater?"

It is impossible to measure the success rate of our actions.

Two Rhino species are present in South Africa, namely the Black and the White Rhino, also known as the Hook Lipped and Square Lipped Rhino, respectively. Since the 1960's, populations of these species in South Africa have made a remarkable comeback thanks to Dr Ian Player.

Elsewhere in Africa and Asia, Rhino populations have plummeted and in most cases become locally extinct. The success in South Africa was mainly due to intensive management and protection, and expanding the range within South Africa to areas where rhinos had disappeared. This success, however, is being rapidly undone before our eyes by the recent onslaught of Rhino Poaching, and their numbers are declining towards extinction.

The effective management of Rhino populations requires certain key elements. An individual based identification system is core to the gathering of vital biological data from ground monitoring, such as movements, home range, birth rate, inter-calving periods, associations and aggression, to name a few. With the recent breakthrough in DNA extraction from Rhino horn, it has also become necessary to add to the Rhino database genetic material collected from live Rhinos as another tool in combating poaching.

The large ears of Rhinos make it the perfect place to mark Rhinos. By cutting small V, or square shapes into the ears at certain positions, gives the Rhino an individual number.

Any observation by monitoring officers of this animal into the future, together with the information that is observed, adds to that biological database.

Due to the costs involved in a Rhino immobilisation for this vital management operation, Pilanesberg Park Management has requested The Pilanesberg Wildlife Trust (PWT) to make this a project of the PWT to ensure that this function continues. The PWT in turn solicits donors to contribute to the project by sponsoring a "hands on" Rhino capture experience where guests actively take part and assist the Vet and Park crew during the operation. Excess funds are utilised for further Rhino Protection Projects through funding of training and equipment, etc..

By sponsoring a Rhino immobilization not only do you get to experience a 'once in a lifetime' event, but you also contribute to the conservation, and furthered protection, of these amazing creatures.

An experienced helicopter pilot, Vet and Park management professionally carry out the Rhino notching operation. The helicopter is used to locate an unmarked Rhino, and is the platform from which the Vet darts the Rhino. The helicopter is also used in guiding the animal to suitable working areas and away from danger.

Once the Rhino is adequately sedated, ground crew and guests move in on foot and carry out the necessary procedures of notching, and DNA collection.

Where possible, guests are requested to assist the Vet and Park Management with the Rhino, under the guidance of the experienced Wildlife Vet and Park staff.

The Rhino's safety, welfare, and dignity, is the priority at all times. The Rhino notching will be halted immediately if the Vet attending to the Rhino decides it is at risk.

This is an amazing experience that you will remember, and cherish, forever! For more information about how you could take part in a rhino notching please visit Pilanesbergwildlifetrust.co.za or Contact Perry Dell at pdell@nwpb.org.za.

*The vet and the pilot take flight in the helicopter and identify a rhino who needs to be notched.*

*Once the rhino is darted the rest of the team follow quickly to reach the rhino and begin the procedure. Cotton wool is pressed into the rhino's ears and the rhino is blindfolded. This is done to reduce the stress caused by being in an unfamiliar situation surrounded by humans.*

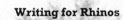

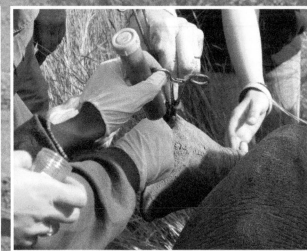

A small piece is cut from the rhino's ear (notched) and DNA is collected. This DNA can be used as evidence if the rhino is poached.

Illustration By: **Joshua Meyer** (South Africa)

# Rhino Checklist

It's always really exciting when you spot a rhino in the wild! Use this checklist to find out a bit more about the rhino you can see.

## Is it a white rhino or a black rhino?

If the rhino has a pointy lip and seems to be browsing on twigs it is a black rhino. White rhinos have a flat, wide lip and they graze on grass.

## Is it a male or a female?

It is really hard to tell the difference without looking at the animal's genitalia but often, the female's horns are longer and thinner while a male's horn is thicker.

## How can you tell the age of a calf?

If the baby rhino's shoulder is in line with the mother's groin the calf is likely to be about 3 months old.

## Has the rhino been notched?

Have a look at the rhino's ear to see if there is a small section cut out. If you see this then it means the rhino has been notched and the conservation team has collected the rhino's DNA.

Illustration By: **Bailey Roberts** (South Africa)

The rhino is big

The rhino is red

The rhino is good

The rhino is small

The rhino is happy

The rhino is black

I like the rhino

By Samson

(United Kingdom)

# TRAINS OF THOUGHT

Written by: **Clara Buxbaum** (Austria, Vienna)

Why? Don't you understand?

Just imagine the pain!

It is not for fun.

There are not many of us left

 It is not for the pleasure of the hunt

And we never did you any wrong


But it gives us bread at the end of the day

Why?

 What else can I do?

We are creatures that feel pain – just like you.

 I don't have a choice.

It does not hold any power

 I need to provide for my family

But leaves orphans behind

And therefore risk my life

This needs to stop!

 I wish I had a choice.

We need to act now!

Who cares about us anyways?

Let us live and survive

 I don't want to kill

Protect us – don't hunt us down.

I want to learn an honest skill.

# Wildlife celebration

**195 countries in the world
seven continents
somewhere in Southern Africa
one of the big five
critically endangered!
Diceros bicornis:
the black rhino
brilliant and bulky
protected by skilled field rangers**

**Come blow the trumpets
and leave the horns,
celebrate with Africa
for another rhino is born!**

**Christél Jordaan**

(South Africa)

# THE HABITAT BATTLE

**Elanie Snyman** (South Africa)

Long, long ago in the open fields, lived two rhino cousins, Blackie and Snow White. One day, Blackie and Snow White had a fight, because both of them wanted to eat from the same bush. Blackie and Snow White pushed and bumped each other. Bam!! Dust was all over the place, but fortunately Snow White and Blackie did not get hurt, because they have thick skin.

Snow White didn't think that Blackie would carry on with the fight, but suddenly Blackie stumbled upon Snow White. Blackie lifted her head up and bumped into Snow White. Snow White tumbled into a hole with her head first.

After the habitat battle, Snow White's face was pointing downwards. Blackie's head was lifted in the air, because she lifted her head to run into Snow White. Snow White didn't want to fight with her cousin anymore. She wanted the habitat battle to end. Snow White and Blackie decided to have a picnic at the dam one night, to end the battle.

To end the battle, both Snow White and Blackie, knew they had to part and live far away from each other, so that there won't be another battle. After having the picnic, the two cousins said goodbye. Blackie swam through the dam, to get across. She struggled, but got safely to the other side.

On Blackie's side, there were lots of bushes and trees. Blackie ate the stems from these trees and bushes. On Snow White's side, there was mostly grass to eat. Snow White could never lift her head up to eat stems from trees and neither could Blackie put her head down to eat grass.

Still today, Blackie's family's head is lifted in the air and they live in bushy habitats with lots of trees and thickets. Snow White's family on the other side, still live in open fields with their heads pointing downwards.

# A NOTE FROM MICHAEL CATTERSON....

Plan a trip to South Africa, book an early morning safari and see if you are lucky enough to spot the Big 4... although this statement sounds incorrect, we are slowly moving towards the reality of "The Big 4" as rhino populations are depleted due to the daily poaching for their horns. Without human intervention, these beautiful animals face extinction and we need to do our bit to contribute towards a solution.

Local South African radio station, Mix FM and the Mix'd Up Breakfast Show, are dedicated to nature conservation and promoting rhino protection is a large part of what can be done to assist in the daily battle. Along with the assistance of Kwa Maritane Bush Lodge in the Pilanesberg Game Reserve, the Mix'dUp Breakfast Show set up occasional bush broadcasts where the entire show is dedicated to raising awareness for these incredible creatures. Despite these bush broadcasts being a lot of fun, it is very important that the presenters do not lose focus and ensure the message is communicated to every listener, just how serious this problem has become. Interviews are set up with several role players in the bush such as the Rhino Protection Unit, The Pilanesberg Wildlife Trust, relevant fund-raising committees, game rangers and even guests who can offer their personal experiences had with these animals.

One memorable experience that I recall was when I was invited to a Rhino notching one early morning in the Pilanesberg Game Reserve. The helicopter went up to search for a specific young rhino and once located, the animal was darted with a temporary tranquiliser, and the action started. The vehicles raced to the site where the Rhino lay sleeping and all the checks were done before notching the Rhino's ear for data collection and tracking purposes. Each guest had the opportunity to have contact with this amazing creature. Once all the interactions and medical work had concluded, the Rhino was woken up with an antidote and the young calf walked away with the sound of a high pitch whine as he called for his mother. It left one thought behind that would never be forgotten, how long would that young animal call for his mother, if his mother was no longer there.

The reality is that young Rhinos are left orphaned after losing their mothers on an almost weekly basis in South Africa and it is up to all of us to do our bit and contribute in some way towards saving this species. By spreading the word to at least one person who had no knowledge of this tragic and regular occurrence, would create the kind of awareness that could contribute just that little bit towards saving our African Rhino.

Michael interviews **Steve Dell**, the field ecologist at Pilanesberg, during a Mix FM bush broadcast

# Reggie the Rhino

## By Millie Jacobs

Reggie the Rhino loves Rugby. Every afternoon in the sun he plays, he thinks about rugby ALL the time and dreams of becoming a great rugby player someday.

### Reggie the Rhino loves rugby

The moment Reggie's mum lays down for a nap in the shade of tree, Reggie is up and running with his rugby ball. He darts this way and that trying to score his best try yet!

One early morning as Reggie laid lazily in the dust, he sneezed

## ahhhhchooooooo !

Blowing up a dust cloud, for a moment he stared, then out of the corner of his eye something moved very quickly. Turning he saw a little grey shape in a dust cloud of its own.

Reggie blinked the shape seemed to hop away behind some tall grass. Racing to his feet Reggie pressed his nose into the grasses. He huffed and puffed, suddenly something grey was on his snout gently taking a step back Reggie looked down his long nose to see a small bunny. 'Agh! Who...w w w what are you?' He blurted out.

The bunny hopped 'I'm Dot a dust bunny, pleased to meet you!' Reggie's jaw dropped 'a what?'

'A dust bunny, you blew me out of the dust when you sneezed' continued Dot

Reggie lowered his head and the dust bunny hopped of the end of his nose turning to hop away 'stop' said Reggie 'I mean wait, do you want to play?'

The dust bunny hoped up and down so quick the dust puffed up all around her 'yes please'

Reggie glanced over the grasses and saw his mum nearby grazing 'wait here' he said. Reggie told his mum he would be playing rugby in the clearing just behind her.

Dot the dust bunny ran in her own dust cloud alongside Reggie.

### Reggie the Rhino loves rugby

Reggie nuzzled his favourite rugby ball out from a tuft of grass 'ready?' he said nose down to the ground.

'ready' said Dot

Reggie snorted, grabbed the ball under his arm and RAN Dot Looked on confused 'I'm going for the try!' shouted Reggie as he thundered towards a line drawn in the dirt 'and he SCORES!!!!' Reggie spun round in the dust 'wooooooooo! yes, yes YES!' he cried and then he saw Dot looking bewildered

'oh' chuckled Reggie 'I'm sorry, we're playing RUGBY it's my favourite. You must run to the try line and score a try, but I can tackle you to stop you, ok?'

Dot Nodded 'let me hold the ball' As soon as Dot Got the ball she tucked it under her arm and ran just like Reggie before. Behind her she heard Reggie spin in the dust and start chasing her. Dot RAN, just before she could reach the try line Reggie caught her 'ha ha got you!' they both rolled on the ground and laughed.

For the rest of the afternoon the friends played. Reggie's mum called softly to him.

'Same time again tomorrow?' asked Reggie looking at Dot 'You bet!' she replied.

Reggie the Rhino loves rugby and now every afternoon he plays with his new best friend.

The end

(South Africa)

# FOREVER

STRONG AND BOLD YOU RUN IN THE WILD
ALWAYS THERE SINCE I WAS A CHILD
PLAY IN THE MUD AND SPLASH IN A POOL
IN YOUR CRASH WHILST THE WORLD BECAME CRUEL

AS TIME PASSES AND PEOPLES HEARTS GREED
THEY CHOSE YOU TO SUFFER AND LEFT YOU TO BLEED

WE STAND TOGETHER AS NATION AND LANDS
OTHER CONTINENTS TAKING OUR HANDS
TO SAVE YOU OUR RHINO OUR BIG FIVE
WE WANT TO SAVE YOU THAT'S WHAT WE STRIVE

PROCLAIMING LIVE OVER YOU AND THE REST
MAY YOU LIVE LONG AND FOREVER BE BLESSED

-CHANTEL ROTTCHER

**Alex Roy** (South Africa)

# UNDER A POACHER'S MOON

Written by **Anne Moth** (United Kingdom)

A tightening lump comes to our throat,
The murderers they just sit and gloat
Looking at the horns they've killed for
Under a poachers moon.
The tears run hot, down each cheek
Another rhino killed this week
Those who care cry with sorrow
Please God, not another tomorrow.
Under a poachers moon.
Will this massacre never cease,
For pity's sake leave them in peace.
But we know there'll be another soon
Under a poachers moon.
Many people love moon light
But wouldn't  if they viewed the sight
Of a rhino dead or maimed at night
Under a poachers moon.
Mother nature, ease the pain
Every month, make it rain and rain
Make the skies the blackest black
So the poachers cannot attack
Under a poachers moon.

Anne Moth. Rhino warrior.

**Emmica Gaspar** (South Africa)

# PLAYING IN THE CLOUDS

One day my friend asked me why I was so upset, it was because a rhino that had touched my heart had been poached, there was silence. I told them about when he was small and he used to play in the grass but now he will only play in the clouds.

The story started one warm African evening when he and his mom were on their way to the water hole for a drink of water. That night an awful sound like thunder and lightning shattered through the air.

Suddenly his mom fell to the ground, it all happened so suddenly.

There were scary looking animals; they came running towards them and his Mom. He tried to fend them off but they hit him with something sharp, he tried again but they hit him again.

He ran off and when he came back, he tried to get his Mom to wake up but she didn't... So he slept next to her to protect her.

In the morning he was so thirsty that he tried to go to the watering hole but he was spotted by some people and they took him to the Rhino Orphanage, where this nice lady became his "Mom". He even had a friend.

When he got too big, he got released back into the wild but he too suffered the same fate as his Mom.

By **Wendy-Kate Lemke**. (South Africa)

# THE K9 UNIT

The Pilanesberg National Park has a dedicated K9 Unit who work alongside The anti-poaching unit. The Pilanesberg Wildlife Trust rely on donations to train the dogs and handlers. Heilie and Russell are the two specially trained K9 unit dogs used in The Pilanesberg. Donations towards the maintenance and wellbeing of these special animals is greatly appreciated.

*The APU with Hendrick and Russel (left)*  *Kobus and Heilie in front of a rhino carcass (right)*

My name is Phoebee Iris Roberts

I am 12 years old and I am in Grade 6.2

Thank you for everything you do with the APU dogs and everything you do to help the fight against Rhino Poaching.
With out people like you our Rhinos have no chance.

SAVE THE RHINO

My name is Baylee Rose Roberts

I am 9 years old, I am in Grade 4.3

My sister and I have a company called Raising Rhinos.
Every day we join the fight to save the Rhinos by helping raise money and awareness for the fight.
We want our children to see Rhinos in the wild one day
Thank you for all your hard work with the APU dogs

# THE RHINO ORPHANAGE

The Rhino Orphanage is the world's first Non-Profit Organization dedicated to the care and rehabilitation of rhino calves orphaned by poaching. The orphanage is located in Limpopo Province, South Africa. This is where orphans of Pilanesberg National Park are relocated to and given a chance at a new life.

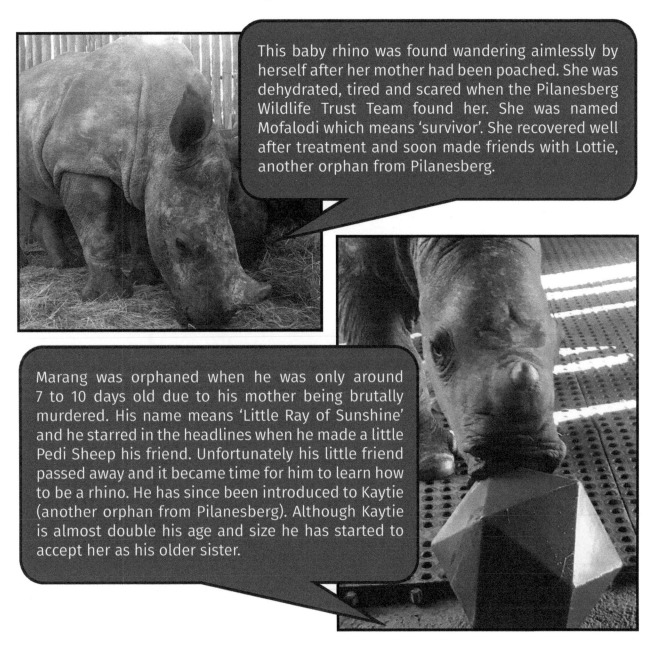

This baby rhino was found wandering aimlessly by herself after her mother had been poached. She was dehydrated, tired and scared when the Pilanesberg Wildlife Trust Team found her. She was named Mofalodi which means 'survivor'. She recovered well after treatment and soon made friends with Lottie, another orphan from Pilanesberg.

Marang was orphaned when he was only around 7 to 10 days old due to his mother being brutally murdered. His name means 'Little Ray of Sunshine' and he starred in the headlines when he made a little Pedi Sheep his friend. Unfortunately his little friend passed away and it became time for him to learn how to be a rhino. He has since been introduced to Kaytie (another orphan from Pilanesberg). Although Kaytie is almost double his age and size he has started to accept her as his older sister.

# A NEW LIFE

The rhino uses the horn to cut the tree. Far, far away in Africa the rhino has a horn but he has no friends. The Rhino is all alone and sad.

He has a new life and he is really big and grey. He loves drinking water from the river. He loves living in Africa. Africa is a wonderful place.

The end

By **Josh** (United Kingdom)

Credit: **The Rhino Orphanage**

# RHINOS MATTER

(extracts from the writing of Lee Dormer Vice Chairman of the Wilderness Leadership School-South Africa and the Pilanesberg Wildlife Trust.)

That evening, sitting in a circle, the children watched as their father prepared a small fire on which to cook the evening meal. A high-pitched squeal caused the children to leap up and turn in unison to stare into the thickets. Their father sternly whispered a warning to stay quiet and still. After checking the direction of the rising smoke to be sure they could not be scented he slowly rose from his haunches. A young Black Rhinoceros stepped into the open area between the thickets and the family group. The wind direction suddenly swirled and the scent of the group reached the rhino which swerved with remarkable agility and bolted back into the dense undergrowth. "That looked like Khutsi" said father. "How wonderful to see him alive and looking so well". The children looked at their father with quizzical expressions. "I'm sorry,Khutsi's story began eighteen months ago".

Father composed himself before starting to speak. "It was early morning and Khutsiwas playing his usual game of fetch and carry. He was bouncing back and forth, picking up sticks with his finger-like lip and tossing them about. Occasionally he would interrupt his game by spinning around and stabbing the air with his small bump of a horn as if attacking an imaginary foe.

Khutsi often entertained himself this way and on this morning he had played until fatigue forced him to collapse against his mother who was resting in the cool shade of a Shepherd's Tree. With the comforting feeling of his mother's body pressed against his, Khutsi fell into an exhausted sleep.

His mother had a placid temperament and was known to be a good parent. She radiated that soul-felt connection with her little boy. Sighing through her nostrils, she shifted her weight in a gesture of love and protectiveness as she firmly wedged their bodies together in the bond only a mother feels for her child.

Remaining alert while Khutsi slept she rotated her ears to activate her acute hearing and continuously scented the air to warn of any threat to her adored son.

The rains had been kind that season, providing an abundance of browsing, and she was content that the coming winter would not be challenging.

Her sense of well-being instantly vaporized with the sound of movement and the chirring of her attendant oxpeckers. She rose to her feet in an instant. Turning, she rushed forward, holding her head high and curling her tail. She began puffing and snorting as she sensed danger was nearby. Straining forward to scent the air she rotated her ears as she desperately sought the source of her agitation. There was no scent or sound as she remained still and glanced at Khutsi's resting form.

Her mind slipped for a brief moment from the present to reflecting on Khutsi and his adorable habit of bumping her head whenever he wished to try and take her depleting milk. At this moment she stiffened and her pulse leapt as her nostrils were filled with the scent of several two-leggeds.

Simultaneously, she heard the wet thud of a bullet penetrating her flesh, the next shattering her knee, and she collapsed onto her chest as more shots rained into her. The searing pain made her giddy and she desperately tried to make sense of what was happening to her.

With great effort driven by her need to save her son she clamoured onto three legs and managed a single pace toward Khutsi who was now on his feet and squealing in deep throated anguish. She collapsed again in intolerable pain. She was weakening rapidly as her life force began draining and Khutsi's squeals were fading as she fought death. She felt the first blow of the axe across her nose. The second blow cut deep into her nasal passages, releasing a fresh flow of blood. Choking in her own blood, her plea was for her son's safety. She didn't feel the axe that hacked at her rear horn. She was gone."

Their father turned away and looked into the sky in a moment of personal grief; he could be heard whispering unintelligible words to the heavens.

Each of the children moved away into personal space as they too wrestled with their emotions.

Blake tended the small fire as a distraction and stared deeply into the small flames, picking up small sticks and clutching them for long periods as he examined each one before offering them to burn.

Barrie-Kim openly wept, her lips scrunched and she blew heavily into a tissue to clear her streaming nose.

Kealan's eyes were shining with moisture and he walked back and forth opening and closing his pen knife in a display of agitation.

Father turned and spoke: "Rhinos have walked the earth for millions of years and can be described as a remaining example of prehistoric times. Their main predator has been man due to the notion that their horn has medicinal properties. The Asian Rhino is all but extinct mainly due to them being murdered for their horn. Once this source of horn was exhausted the poachers moved into Africa and have steadily murdered their way down the continent and now they are here in South Africa where the bulk of the remaining populations of Black and White Rhino remain. The truth is that the horn is made up of a protein called Keratin, the same as your fingernails and it has no medicinal benefit at all. However, there are people from consumer countries in the East that believe otherwise. Today the value of the horn has created a new demand and wealthy people desire to give it as a gift to those they want to impress and acknowledge as important to them. This illusionary esteem value combined with the belief in its medicinal power is the driving force that is callously murdering rhino. I am appalled at the senseless greed-driven murder of the Rhino. If we don't find a solution then the Rhino will be gone forever. Each day we lose species of animals, insects, plants and trees which will ultimately harm our life support system, only to satisfy a few greedy people and to feed what are thought to be needs. We all have a responsibility to see that we beat this evil by getting involved to grow consciousness and change the beliefs that fuel this carnage. We need a value system, an ethic that guides humans to respect all life in the same way that they value their own.

Many years ago an American Indian named Chief Seattle spoke of the importance of respecting all life. He said, "What is man without the animals? If all the animals are gone, man would die of a great loneliness of spirit. For whatever happens to the animals will soon happen to man. All things are connected, this we know. The earth does not belong to man, man belongs to the earth."

The children gathered closer to their father as he continued talking.

"Khutsi's mum was the first Rhino in this reserve to be murdered for her horn. As a critically endangered Black Rhino her death has been a devastating blow to the conservation effort and a sad indictment of the lack of ethics amongst some humans.

When her baby was robbed of his mother we decided to name him Khutsi from the Tswana "Khutsana" meaning orphan. Whenever we are in the area in which the murder took place we keep a look out for Khutsi. He has become the inspiration for us to double our efforts to protect the Rhinos here from being harmed. He has symbolized hope and his story has motivated everyone. At such a young age we wondered if he would adapt and find enough food, every sighting of him is a reminder to us all of the need to persevere."

Blake asked "tell us another story?"

"I think you should have your own direct experience of the power of nature and the potential it has to affect your lives."

Sweeping his arms as a gesture to mark out an area of the grassland adjoining the fireplace and temporary kitchen their father spoke. "At this time of the year the grasses are pregnant with seed. This makes it easier to compare and identify the different grasses. If you are willing, I would like to ask that each of you independently find as many different grasses as possible without going beyond the boundaries I pointed out. The winner will be excused from any camp duties for the remainder of our stay here."

Rushing around as though they had been released onto a playground the youngsters threw themselves into the task. Breaking off the seed heads of the different grasses they clutched them like a bunch of flowers. A few minutes later their father called "Time". Each was asked to count their harvest. Kealan announced with a measure of pride, "I have got ten grasses". Having declared his hand he strained his head to see behind the backs of the others who had chosen to hide their spoils.

Blake grinned broadly and blurted in the tone of a poker player "Hey Kea! I will see you and raise you one."

In keeping with her quiet and bashful good nature Barrie-Kim smiled and shyly said "I think I have eleven but I may have counted some more than once."

With that she withdrew her arm from behind her back and handed her collection of grasses to her father for approval.

"This grass is known as Spear Grass or Heteropogon Contortus, we use the common name to make it easy to remember. If you look closely you can see the spear point and barb of the seed head which explains how it was given its name. If I wet the shaft that holds the seed you can see how it rotates or contorts as the shaft dries out. Little wonder how "contortus" found its way into the scientific name." The children leaned forward exclaiming their fascination and interest as each plucked a seed shaft to wet in their mouths. "This guy likes soils that drain well and if you look at the ground where this patch is growing you will notice it is more gravel than fine soil. In the early summer when it is generating new growth I have often seen the Sable Antelope feeding on this grass. This is because it is most palatable in a growth phase. The presence of this grass is an indication that there has been a disturbance to the soil and these guys are very useful in the way they germinate in open areas to hold the soil together. As the soil condition changes into the future they will give way to other grasses that are better suited for the new conditions."

Selecting the next one, father smiled broadly at the children. "This is called Love Grass (Eragrostis Superba) because of the heart shaped seed. The serrated edges tell us that it is the Saw-Tooth variety of Love Grass. It also grows in sandy or gravel type soil and is very talented at rehabilitating bare patches of ground to hold onto our precious soil. It is highly nutritious and readily eaten by grazing animals, it grows really quickly and this guy is resilient in times of drought. All in all, this grass has such wonderful attributes and plays a vital role in the life of the earth and all of us who live on the planet."

Blake commented "Gee Dad, you speak about the grass like you would about people!"

"To me they should have as much right to life as we do. They are a vital component of the essence of our existence, they sustain us and I have the most profound respect for them. Wherever I may be the grass is always present and I greet them as I would a brother. It delights me when traveling the roads to look out for who is living by the roadside and beyond. I have the same experience with the trees. To me the plants, animals, birds and insects are extended family and I would not harm them consciously. If you nurture a curious mind and you take those moments to explore you will discover the beauty and interconnectedness with all life. It is so hard to imagine our lives without the grasses. You only have to think about what you eat each day."

Barrie-Kim commented "I guess the meat we eat is because the animals depend on the grasses.". "Absolutely," replied Dad, "That leads on to a whole new conversation: The growing human population has placed a greater demand on meat production and the available grass to sustain the number of animals required. So much so that more and more domestic livestock no longer live a natural life. They are being kept in confined spaces and fed alternative foods. I, for one, am abhorred by this and only buy what today is referred to as organic meat. I pay more for this but at least I am assured that the meat was grass fed and lived a more natural and authentic life. Equally I am eating less meat and on moral grounds thinking that I should stop altogether." Pausing to allow the weight of his words to be absorbed the children's father went on.

"Barrie-Kim is right; our meat, eggs, milk, cereal, bread and butter and more come from the grass. We are indeed sustained by the grass!

Always remember that the grasses also protect the nutrient rich top soil against the effects of rain and wind. Without being noticed they work away for the benefit of all, fertilizing, feeding and protecting, they deserve our care, appreciation and respect."

One by one the children were introduced to the remaining grasses that Barrie-Kim had found, Thatching Grass (Hyparrhenia hirta) Red Grass (Themeda triandra) Three-awn (Aristida congesta) Natal Red Top (Melenis repens) Couch Grass (Cynodon dactylon) Wire Grass (Elionurus muticus) Pin Hole Grass (Bothriochloa insculpta) Ratstail Grass (Sporobolus africanus) and Finger Grass (Digitaria eriantha)

Barrie-Kim was the first to break the silence that ensued. "I feel so humbled by this experience, it amazes me that I was so blind to the fact that there are so many different grasses and that they are so important to all of us.I am astounded that the food I consume every-day and take for granted is either grass or derived from grass. I for one will never look at grass the same way."

"Until you have had your own direct experience then nothing is entirely real. We have walked all day in the presence of these life giving plants without giving them any notice. Perhaps the only time that we become aware of them is when being aggravated by the discomfort of some seeds that get tangled in our clothing. It could be said that because they are always present we actually stop seeing them, that they disappear from our minds to the extent that they become an invisible part of the larger landscape and as such no longer noticed. In much the same way we have become detached from the planet because we do not see what the earth means to us and stopped seeing the gift of life it gives us.

Think about the many people in our lives that are ever present but not acknowledged or perhaps not understood. Who is the grass in your life? Who are the least respected people that have a role in your eco-system? Think of the people who fulfill a role in your life but may not be seen consciously to do so. Can you think of those people? Do you know anything about them? Do you acknowledge them and the value they bring to you? What are their dreams and aspirations? What of your friends and family members?

Grass has the most resilient nature, it can be cut, torn or burnt and yet this only serves to stimulate it to get stronger. This in itself is a powerful metaphor for all who choose to see the message and embrace it in their approach to the challenges that we all inevitably face in life.

In the same way that grass fulfils its role in your eco-system there are people who turn up each day, often despite challenges, so that they can fulfill a role for you. Look for these people and make it your mission to learn something about them and be certain to acknowledge the value they bring to you. This is respectfulness in action."

*I wonder how many people see the earth as a living being that is host to millions of other life forms, each depending on the other and interacting in a complex web that ultimately makes our own lives possible.*

*Our human experience and view of the world is influenced by our cultures and traditions. This has fundamental difficulties associated to it, no more so than in the context of our modern lives. Our need to consume has overwhelmed the earth's capacity to meet our ever increasing demands of her. The illusionary lifestyles we are programmed to aspire to live has caused us to become disconnected from the basic biology of our living planet.*

*The beliefs and resultant behaviours that flow from our illusionary lives dramatically influences how we conduct ourselves in our relationships with people, the earth and the beings that surround us. The very notion that we have dominance or custodianship over the planet places us above it and as such separate from it. Our lives depend on the earth giving of itself to feed our many illusionary needs when all that we truly need is fresh air, nourishing food and potable water. Each of these basic needs are under threat as humans drive unconsciously and relentlessly to own and demand those things that will disable a sustainable human future. When a critical mass of people stop living the illusion and begin to understand that we are one species in a larger community, only then we will cease to forfeit our ability to have a future.*

*Take a moment and imagine a council of beings assembled to express their view on the value of humans. Would they currently acknowledge us as contributing to a healthy living planet or would they have cause to fear us?*

*We have no other means of existence than that which the earth's grace gives us.*

*An earth that relies on the order of things, an order that in many ways is still a great mystery to us. One thing I am certain of is that the respect for all life is the human ingredient that is missing to balance the order for a sustainable human earth life.Only then will the senseless murder and exploitation of our natural world resources cease.*

# THE BLACK RHINO

One sunny day the Black Rhino was having fun with his friends. He told his friends that he always wanted to go to space so they played a space game. The Black Rhino was the driver and did a good job on controlling the Rhino Rocket.

When they finished the game, they made a secret plan to actually go to space. The rhinos worked together to build an epic rocket (called 'The Rhino Rocket'). They made their plans to keep the rocket secret. When all of them were on the Rhino Rocket, the Black Rhino pressed the 'go up' button excitedly and off they flew. The fire-breathing engine was roaring as the rocket blasted into space.

First they visited the cool Space Station which was filled with famous scientists. Next, they landed at their destination. The rhinos got off the rocket and walked on the dark moon. It felt amazing. It felt like riding a hover-board. When it was time to go home they were exhausted. The three rhinos got into the rocket and flew home. When they were home, all three of them hid the rocket and looked forward to being an astronaut.

Nineteen years later, the rhinos were real astronauts and were very famous. They invented a rocket which goes 9000 mph and found a space storm which they discovered (a space thing that sucks you in). The three rhinos had such fun walking on the moon and making the International Space Station bigger. Their discovery was revealed in the world record book. The rhinos were so famous that they won a Nobel Prize for Science.

By **Tim Aghbosh** (United Kingdom)

# SYNOPSIS: RINTY AND THE RHINO POACHERS.

**Dale Allen** (South Africa)

Rinty, a loveable and highly intelligent Labrador cross border collie, with a quirky sense of humour, looks as if he's about to be abandoned. After three years of carefree living on a small-holding just outside Johannesburg it appears as if his idyllic lifestyle is about to come to an abrupt end.

Fortunately, fate steps in, in the form of Karl, a young tracker employed by the Rhino Protection Foundation, who is searching for talented and trainable young dogs to work in the bushveld helping to apprehend the ruthless poachers who are decimating the country's Rhino population.

Karl sees the potential in Rinty and decides to take him under his wing and put him through the  program for the anti poaching unit under his command.

There, Rinty meets Ajax, a German Shepherd cross Rotweiler, an experienced and battle hardened veteran of many encounters with poachers. Head of the squad  Nanthi, a young game ranger who has sworn to protect, not only Rhino but all endangered wildlife. Also part of Nanthi's squad are two *boerboels*,  Dozer and Falco, who provide much needed "muscle" to the team.(Boerboels are very large dogs, usually guard dogs)

After his initiation into the realities of tracking poachers, and  under the watchful eye of his mentor Nanthi  as well as the bush savvy of Ajax, Rinty discovers the significance of their motto. " Loyalty-Courage- Comradeship." He also learns and appreciates the value of interaction between the many other species living in the bushveld, Elephants, giraffes, lions, zebras, many different types of buck, the various kinds of birds and reptiles, large and small. As Ajax says to him. 'If you just go on about your business most of the other animals will leave you be, but keep an eye out for hyenas, some snakes and crocodiles when you're near the river.'

The events involving the team are hectic, sometimes hilarious, and varied, hardly a day or night goes by without some contact or incident involving poachers taking place. Nanthi and his four dogs have become a much admired and respected squad within the anti poaching fraternity.

In the ongoing fight against the scourge of Rhino and Wildlife poaching, Rinty acquires some new and valuable allies, Mojo, the black leopard, Smug, Shy the pangolin's brother, Cabanga, the Eagle owl and Copper, a young red setter.

With Mojo's help, they uncover a vast smuggling operation involving Rhino horn, Elephant tusks and a host of wildlife skins. Nanthi, Rinty, his old comrades, Ajax, Dozer and Falco set out to catch the smugglers and the kingpins behind this deadly trade.

Daily, our intrepid Wilderness Warriors continue against the odds. Danger lurks at every turn, never has their motto, "Loyalty, Courage, Comradeship" been more tested.

**Dale Allen is a writer from South Africa. He has written a full length story about Rinty and his efforts to fight rhino poaching. This is the synopsis, however if you would like to read the full story please contact us via our facebook page or email us at savingthepilanesberg rhinos@gmail.com.**

Illustration B: **Sradha Vadher**

Once upon a time there was a rhino named Casey. She was a very lonely and sad rhino because the poachers took her mommy, daddy and sister.

She was walking to the dam all on her own.

There was a big elephant named Mila also drinking water.

Casey asked Mila to be her friend.

The elephant said 'Yes, I will be your best friend forever'.

The End.

**Abigail Botha** (South Africa)

I have a great sorrow
For the children of tomorrow
For creatures their eyes will not see.
Lions and tigers, elephants and rhinos
None of them roaming or free.
All because some people prefer to see them dead
Hanging up as trophies, just wanting to use their head
We are just sporting hunters, they say with a grin
They are just dumb animals, they can't see any sin
So heartless and so greedy, no hearts that truly feel
No shame in all the killing of creatures that are real.
So because of men like these the animals continue to die
Never really replenished, although some of us do try
To speak for all the  creatures who do not have a choice
But needless to say we're not winning, we do not have enough voice
So the killings just go on and on and to our great sorrow
They will not be seen by the children of tomorrow.

Anne Moth, Rhino warrior.

# THE FLYING AIRPLANE RHINO

Once there was a rhino

And she loved flying like an airplane.

Her friends came with her.

One day she wanted to go fly but her friends did not want to fly every day. They said no but she asked every day.

They always said no. So she went to fly by herself. She landed on a beautiful island and it was so beautiful that she never wanted to bring her friends to fly ever again. She searched around the island and saw a glowing flower and it glowed so much that she really wanted to keep it. She picked the flower and never showed it to her friends. She brought it every day on her flights. When she flew to the island again she saw more flowers growing and she picked some more.

The end

By **Roxana Aghbosh** (United Kingdom)

Credit: **Perry Dell**

# ROLINDA THE RHINO

There is an animal, who lived not too far away,
Who loves grass, and sunshine, and playing all day.

He is a strange sight, of that you can be sure.
He has a big horn, grey skin and horse ears - it really is obscure.

He roamed the plains of Africa carefree, not long ago,
His name is Rolinda, and he is a rhino.

Rolinda had a mommy, not unlike your own.
And with his mommy, Rolinda never felt scared or alone.

He would eat grass all day and sleep in the shade.
And mommy would come looking for him, hiding in the glade.

"You can't eat and sleep all day, my boy", his mommy would say.
"Or you will be too fat and lazy to run quickly away."

"Run away? Run away from what?" Rolinda cried.
"We're big, tough and strong - even the lions step aside!"
"The crocs, leopards and hyenas don't scare me," Rolinda proclaimed.
"Our horns always keep us safe - why must I be ashamed?"

"The animal we must fear has no horn, fang or claw," mommy said.
"It needs no deer, giraffe, grass or rhino in order to be fed."
"But we must run, as fast as the wind goes,"
"For they want the very thing we cherish, the horn upon our nose."

Rolinda scoffed, sat down, and ate some more grass.
Why would he ever need to run so fast?
He played all day and chased some birds.
And took a nap watching the kudo herds.

But later that day, Rolinda heard a twig crack.
He woke up, rolled over and got up off his back.
A strange creature appeared from behind the tree,
Holding a big grey stick, that made Rolinda want to flee.

Rolinda was scared, he didn't know why.
He really wished that rhinos could fly.
The creature took aim, and revealed a grin.
Rolinda closed his eyes and shivered in his skin.
All of a sudden there was a loud bang.
But the shot didn't hit him, Rolinda's ears just rang.
The creature had somehow missed, oh what a joy!
Mommy had come back to save her little boy.

She rushed at the creatures who ranged one to three,
"This one's is even bigger!" the creatures shrieked with glee.
Mommy slammed two aside, and looked at the other.
Who now had his stick pointed at Rolinda's mother.

Mommy looked at Rolinda, as a tear ran down her eye.
"Run my boy, run as if you could fly!"
Rolinda ran, and ran as fast as can be.
He only stopped when a loud bang rang through the trees.

He turned around and looked to the sky.
Birds were flying away from where he used to lie.
Rolinda looked around and back with despair.
Surely mommy would come out of the grass over there?

He waited and waited until the day got cold.
How could he be left alone, he wasn't that old?
Rolinda was scared, lonely and began to cry.
Where was mommy to sing him a lullaby?

Rolinda turned and ran until his legs couldn't anymore,
His back felt heavy, and his feet were sore.
He lay down to rest in the savannah that night.
No mommy, no sunshine and no will to fight.

The next morning he awoke, a strange sound in the air.
Rolinda looked around quickly, he looked everywhere.
The sound got louder, a sound he never heard.
The creatures were back - this time in a strange, shiny bird.

Rolinda was afraid, he didn't know what to do.
How could he outrun something that flew?
He let out a cry as he saw their grey sticks.
He stood his ground, his eyes were fixed.

As the creatures fired with a dark grey smoke,
Rolinda felt sore on his side, a very sharp poke.
He charged away as fast as he could.
But he was getting slower, from where he last stood.
With every step his legs grew weaker.
His eyes grew heavy and his cries were meeker.

As he slowed down, everything went black.
It was a weird sense of relief, since his mommy's attack.
The last thing he saw, before he went to sleep
Was the bird landing nearby, the creatures beginning to sneak.

Rolinda dreamt of mommy, her horn so great.
And wondered what had become of her and his fate.
He dreamt, so sweetly, of playing in the sun
Eating long grass, and having fun.

When he awoke, there were no creatures.
Only grass, hills and unfamiliar features.
He looked around, confused and groggy.
He was sad - but then he saw mommy!

His heart filled with joy, as he ran to his mom.
He missed her love, it had felt like so long.
Mommy embraced him, but something was gone.
Her head looked sore, something was wrong.

Rolinda looked at his mommy, he felt forlorn.
"Mommy, are you ok? Where is your horn?"
"The bad creatures took it, but it's ok"
"Mommy loves you, mommy is here to stay."

Rolinda thought back to the creatures that night,
And how mommy had attacked and about the big fight.
"But mommy the creatures got me, how did we end up here?"
"My boy, don't worry - you need not fear."

"The creatures got me too, but not the same ones."
"They made me fall with rifles and pistols and all kinds of guns."
"They had a blade, and took my horn."
"They left me on the ground, hurt and torn."
"But just as I thought all was gone."
"Some other creatures arrived with lights that shone."
"They took me away to this here plain,"
"They bandaged my wounds and took away my pain."

Rolinda was happy, he ran around.
He couldn't believe his mother was found.
The dart prick in his side was starting to heal,
And there was plenty of grass to make his meal.

He couldn't believe that the creatures could make him so sad,
But others had saved them - they couldn't all be bad.

Rolinda and his mom were never alone again,
They lived together, and played many a game.
The good creatures took care of them, and many that came after.
And to this day, Rolinda knows nothing but laughter.

Written By **Mark Brown** (South Africa)

# THE INVISIBLE RHINO

Once there lived a rhino who was invisible and not a single animal or

person could see him. One sunny morning he saw another rhino in danger so he saved him and they became friends.

The other rhino said 'I think you are telling a lie, to prove it I'll grab your arm and if you can see me it mean's I am telling a lie'. When the rhino did that, the other rhino did not see him. He painted the rhino grey so he was not invisible anymore but the rain washed it off. When he painted the rhino again the rain did not wash it off. And they lived happily ever after.

The end

by **Parisa Aghbosh** (United Kingdom)

Illustration by **Sophia Aghbosh, Alma and Mitra Valsa**

# ALL ABOUT ME.

I am one of the two species of rhinos. Compared to my cousin the white rhino, I am quite small. I live in Africa, My diet consist of about 40% grass and 60% twigs, leaves and small branches.

I don't really like a human because humans will shoot some sharp things at me, I will pass out one minute and the next my horn is gone.

I think some humans are quite dumb because they think the difference between my cousin, the white rhino is that I am black and they are white...But the difference is quite big, I have a beak like lip which I use to pick small branches and leaves from the trees whereas, the white rhino has a flat wide lip to graze on grass.

Did you know, throughout the world, there are five types of rhino but in Africa there are only two?!

By **Tatum van Breda** (South Africa)

# JACK THE RHINO

Once upon a time. Jack, the little rhino was looking for his mum. Jack was alone and scared.

He got lost. Jack couldn't find his way home.

A rhino poacher saw Jack. The poacher took Jack.

Jack's mum was angry because she had lost Jack.

Now, Jack's mum is protecting all the rhinos to stop any person taking them again.

**David, Deividas, Hinata, Catalin, Andre** (United Kingdom)

**Daniel Meyer** (South Africa)

# WHAT CAN YOU DO TO HELP? HOW CAN YOU MAKE A DIFFERENCE?

## Create awareness !!!

You can tell your friends and family about what is happening to our rhinos. The more people who know what is happening, the more people can help us put an end to the suffering.

Get your school or business to take part in WEAR RED FOR RHINOS on 22 September and if you can, encourage everyone to make a small donation to anti-poaching efforts. When somebody notices that there are a lot of people wearing red they may want to know more about why, tell them!

Join the Global March for Elephants and rhinos. This march takes place all over the world and attracts a lot of attention. I have personally participated in the Johannesburg march and the London march. Crowds of people standing together for a cause such as this creates a huge amount of awareness and this is what we need!

Contact your local radio station and ask them to talk about rhino poaching and what people can do to help.

Donate to an organisation, such as The Pilanesberg Wildlife Trust, who helps to protect our rhinos.

### Organise a fundraiser!!!

Use your special talent or interest to raise funds to support rhino protection efforts. There is always a big need for gear such as boots, cameras and night vision goggles and funds are always greatly appreciated. If you are an excellent baker, host a bake sale. If you are really good at making jewellery or art, sell your work to raise funds. In the past I have hosted family events involving games and dance. Sell the entrance tickets for a small fee and make that your donation. The opportunities are endless!

# WEAR RED FOR RHINOS
# 22 SEPTEMBER

Wear Red For Rhinos is an initiative started in South Africa in 2016. The 22nd of September has been declared World Rhino Day and what a perfect day to wear red to show your support against rhino poaching!

The idea is for schools and businesses to take part in this initiative by encouraging pupils and employees to WEAR RED on World Rhino Day. Individuals and organizations can create awareness by sharing information with others about what is happening to our rhinos. Participants contribute donations to The Pilanesberg Wildlife Trust (via their website or facebook page) to facilitate the protection of our rhinos. Donations made go to the Rhino Protection Unit, without them our rhinos have no protection against the poachers.

In 2018 we saw the initiative grow when people from America and The United Kingdom joined South Africans in WEARING RED FOR RHINOS on World Rhino Day. We look forward to making this a **worldwide** initiative!

Join us on the 22nd of September and WEAR RED FOR RHINOS. Photos can be sent to savingthepilanesbergrhinos@gmail.com and will be published on our facebook page.

# THE STORY BEHIND OUR RHINO MASCOT, STEVE

Donna is a young lady who has always been passionate about the conservation of the rhinos in the Pilanesberg National Park. Christmas of 2015, her brother, Mark, bought her a rhino plush toy. This rhino was by no means small and Donna and husband, Darryn, were moving to the UK in July 2016. She named him Steve and decided his home would be in South Africa. Now if you visit the Pilanesberg National Park and see a whole bunch of people outside the Pilanesberg Centre (PC), selling all sorts of things, you may see Steve the Rhino. Many people have had their photo taken with Steve and with their permission have been published on the Saving the Pilanesberg Rhino and Pilanesberg Wildlife Trust facebook pages.

The people selling items outside PC are volunteers who raise funds for The Pilanesberg Wildlife Trust (PWT). 100% of all money raised is used to support rhino protection efforts in the park.

If you happen to be in the Pilanesberg National Park, pop by and meet Steve.........

By **Beverley Brown**